LEADER GUIDE

For His Glory

LIVING AS GOD'S MASTERPIECE

MARIAN JORDAN ELLIS

Abingdon Women ✳ Nashville

JENNY YOUNGMAN, CONTRIBUTOR

FOR HIS GLORY

Living as God's Masterpiece
Leader Guide

ISBN 978-1-5018-8870-0

Contents

ABOUT THE AUTHOR

Marian Jordan Ellis is a Bible teacher at heart who is passionate about Jesus and helping women of all ages and stages of life to experience the victorious Christian life. Having a Master's Degree in Biblical Studies from Southwestern Baptist Theological Seminary, she served on the teaching team at Second Baptist Church of Houston for fifteen years and now hosts a monthly gathering for hundreds of women at Mission City Church in San Antonio, where she serves as the Director of Women's Ministry. Marian is the founder of This Redeemed Life, a global movement of women transformed by the grace and truth of Jesus Christ. She speaks domestically and internationally at women's conferences and events and has led teaching tours to Israel. Through her evangelistic event, Girls Night Out, she partnered with CRU (Campus Crusade for Christ) and spoke at 170 universities across America where over 11,000 women placed faith in Christ. Marian has been featured on many programs, radio shows, and podcasts including The 700 Club, The Harvest Show, Moody Radio, and FamilyLife Today. Thousands watch her Bible teachings and read her blog each week

on the This Redeemed Life app, website (thisredeemedlife.org), and YouTube channel. She is the author of *Stand: Rising Up Against Darkness, Temptation, and Persecution* and numerous other titles. Marian and her husband, Justin, have three children (Andrew, Brenden, and Sydney) and one very spoiled dog, London.

Follow Marian:

@marianjordan

@marianjordanellis

 thisredeemedlife.org

INTRODUCTION

Have you ever been captivated by a beautiful masterpiece, something that fills you with wonder and leaves you in awe of its creator? We've all likely had that experience at one time or another. But have you ever considered that *you are a masterpiece*? *It's true!*

Ephesians unashamedly declares that the church is God's masterpiece—and because we are the church, that includes you and me. In Christ Jesus, we are transformed from death to life, from broken to beautiful, from rejected to chosen, from alienated to family, from defeated to victorious, from lost to redeemed. In Him we become God's masterpiece—all for the glory of His name!

This one word, *masterpiece*, encompasses the breathtaking beauty of this epistle, or letter, of the apostle Paul and the purpose for which it was penned. Paul longed to convey to the church in Ephesus the mystery and majesty of God's glorious purpose for their lives—and the lives of all believers through the ages. It is a plan that began before the foundation of the world and involves each person of the Trinity: Father, Son, and Holy Spirit. God's magnificent design was and is to redeem a people for Himself who reflect His glory to the world—who are His masterpiece.

If the Bible contains a "how-to" manual for living the Christian life, I suggest it is Ephesians. In this succinct yet powerful epistle we find the key doctrines of the Christian faith. *For His Glory: Living as God's Masterpiece* is a six-week study of Ephesians that helps us understand the glory of God revealed in the gospel, equips us with a clear understanding of our identity in Christ as believers, and empowers each of us to live a life worthy of our Redeemer—to live as God's masterpiece for His glory.

As you lead a group in this journey, my desire is that each of you will be awestruck by the beauty, majesty, and glory of God; that you will be undone with love for Jesus; and that you will overflow with gratitude as you behold the Father's incredible plan to redeem and restore you to Himself. This glorious plan, called the gospel, is perhaps most clearly taught and explained in Ephesians; and my earnest prayer as you and your group faithfully examine its words is that you are transformed into the masterpiece God intends you to be!

About the Participant Workbook

In the introductory session, distribute copies of the participant workbook to the members of your group. This session is a gathering to distribute books, get to know one another, have a brief discussion, and watch the video in preparation for the first week of lessons. For each week there are five lessons that follow an inductive Bible study technique asking the following questions along the way: *What does it say? What does it mean? How does it apply to my life?* Each reading can be completed in about twenty to thirty minutes. Completing these lessons each week will prepare the women for the discussion and activities of the group session.

About This Leader Guide

As you gather each week with the members of your group, you will have the opportunity to watch a video, discuss and respond to what you're learning, and pray together. You will need access to a television and a DVD player with working remotes.

Creating a warm and inviting atmosphere will help make the women feel welcome. Although optional, you might consider providing snacks for your first meeting and inviting group members to rotate in bringing refreshments each week.

This Leader Guide and the DVD will be your primary tools for leading each group session. In this book you will find outlines for an introductory session and six group sessions, each formatted for either a 60-minute or 90-minute group session:

60-Minute Format
Leader Prep (Before the Session)
Welcome and Opening Prayer   *2 minutes*
Icebreaker   *3 minutes*
Group Discussion   *20 minutes*
Video / Brief Discussion   *30 minutes*
Closing Prayer   *5 minutes*

90-Minute Format

Leader Prep (Before the Session)

Welcome and Opening Prayer	2 minutes
Icebreaker	3 minutes
Group Discussion	35 minutes
Deeper Conversation	10 minutes
Video / Brief Discussion	35 minutes
Closing Prayer	5 minutes

As you can see, the 90-minute format is identical to the 60-minute format but has more time for group discussion plus a deeper conversation exercise for small groups. Feel free to adapt or modify either of these formats, as well as the individual segments and activities, in any way to meet the specific needs and preferences of your group.

Here is a brief overview of the elements included in both formats:

Leader Prep
(Before the Session)

For your preparation prior to the group session, this section provides an overview of the week's theme, the main point of the session, key Scriptures, and a list of materials and equipment needed. Be sure to review this section, as well as the session outline, before the group to plan and prepare. If you choose, you also may find it helpful to watch the DVD segment in advance.

Welcome and Opening Prayer
(2 minutes)

To create a warm, welcoming environment as the women are gathering before the session begins, consider lighting one or more candles, providing coffee or other refreshments, and/or playing worship music. (Bring an iPod, smartphone, or tablet and a portable speaker if desired.) Be sure to provide name tags if the women do not know one another or you have new participants in your group. Then, when you are ready to begin, read aloud the thematic prayer that is provided (repeating it each week), or offer your own prayer. You also may find it helpful to read aloud the Overview found in the Leader Prep section if not all group members have completed their homework.

Icebreaker
(3 minutes)

Use the icebreaker to briefly engage the women in the topic while helping them feel comfortable with one another.

Group Discussion (20–40 minutes, depending on session length)

To review the weekly lessons, choose from the questions provided to facilitate group discussion. You may choose to read aloud the discussion points—which are excerpts from the participant workbook—or express them in your own words; then use one or more of the questions that follow to guide your conversation.

Note that more material is provided than you will have time to include. Before the session, select what you want to cover, putting a check mark beside it in your book. Reflect on each question and make some notes in the margins to share during your discussion time. Page references are provided for those questions that relate to specific questions or activities in the participant workbook. For these questions, invite group members to turn in their workbooks to the pages indicated. Participants will need Bibles in order to look up various supplementary Scriptures.

Depending on the number of women in your group and the level of their participation, you may not have time to cover everything you have selected, and that is okay. Rather than attempting to bulldoze through, follow the Spirit's lead and be open to where the Spirit takes the conversation. Remember that your role is not to have all the answers but to encourage discussion and sharing.

Deeper Conversation (10 minutes)

If your group is meeting for 90 minutes, move next to this exercise for deeper sharing in small groups, dividing into groups of two or three. This is a time for women to share more intimately and build connections with one another. (Encourage the women to break into different groups each week.) Before the session, write the question or questions you want to discuss on a markerboard or chart paper for all to see. Give a two-minute warning before time is up so that the groups may wrap up their discussion.

Video / Brief Discussion (30 minutes)

Next, watch the next week's video segment together. Be sure to direct participants to the Video Viewer Guide in the participant workbook, which they may complete as they watch the video. (Answers are provided on page 59 in this book and page 207 in the participant workbook.) Following the video, choose one or two discussion questions to briefly share thoughts or highlights from the video.

Closing Prayer (5 minutes)

Close by leading the group in prayer. Invite the women to briefly name prayer requests. To get things started, you might share a personal request of your own. As women share their requests, model for the group by writing each request in your participant workbook, indicating that you will remember to pray for them during the week.

As the study progresses, you might encourage members to participate in the Closing Prayer by praying out loud for each other and for the requests given. Ask the women to volunteer to pray for specific requests, or have each woman pray for the woman on her right or left. Make sure name tags are visible so that group members do not feel awkward if they do not remember someone's name.

After the prayer, remind the women to pray for one another throughout the week.

Before You Begin

[23] Peace to the brothers and sisters, and love with faith from God the Father and the Lord Jesus Christ. [24] Grace to all who love our Lord Jesus Christ with an undying love.

(EPHESIANS 6:23-24 NIV)

Yes, peace to you dear sisters. May the God of our Lord Jesus Christ reveal to you that you are indeed a masterpiece on display for His glory!

Preparing for the Sessions

❖ Decide whether you will use the 60-minute or 90-minute format option. Be sure to communicate dates and times to participants in advance.

❖ Distribute participant workbooks to all members during your introductory session. If you have the phone numbers or email addresses of your group members, send out a reminder and a welcome.

❖ Check out your meeting space before each group session. Make sure the room is ready. Do you have enough chairs? Do you have the equipment and supplies you need? (See the list of materials needed in each session outline.)

❖ Pray for your group and each group member by name. Ask God to work in the life of every woman in your group.

❖ Read and complete the week's lessons in the participant workbook and review the session outline in the Leader Guide. Select the discussion points and questions you want to cover and make some notes in the margins to share in your discussion time.

Leading the Sessions

❖ Personally welcome and greet each woman as she arrives. Take attendance if desired.

❖ At the start of each session, ask the women to turn off or silence their cell phones.

❖ Always start on time. Honor the time of those who are on time.

❖ Encourage everyone to participate fully, but don't put anyone on the spot. Invite the women to share as they are comfortable. Be prepared to offer a personal example or answer if no one else responds at first.

�֎ Communicate the importance of completing the weekly lessons and participating in group discussion.

✤ Facilitate but don't dominate. Remember that if you talk most of the time, group members may tend to listen rather than to engage. Your task is to encourage conversation and keep the discussion moving.

✤ If someone monopolizes the conversation, kindly thank her for sharing and ask if anyone else has any insights.

✤ Try not to interrupt, judge, or minimize anyone's comments or input.

✤ Remember that you are not expected to be the expert or have all the answers. Acknowledge that all of you are on this journey together, with the Holy Spirit as your leader and guide. If issues or questions arise that you don't feel equipped to handle or answer, talk with the pastor or a staff member at your church.

✤ Don't rush to fill the silence. If no one speaks right away, it's okay to wait for someone to answer. After a moment, ask, "Would anyone be willing to share?" If no one responds, try asking the question again a different way—or offer a brief response and ask if anyone has anything to add.

✤ Encourage good discussion, but don't be timid about calling time on a particular question and moving ahead. Part of your responsibility is to keep the group on track. If you decide to spend extra time on a given question or activity, consider skipping or spending less time on another question or activity in order to stay on schedule.

✤ Try to end on time. If you are running over, give members the opportunity to leave if they need to. Then wrap up as quickly as you can.

✤ Thank the women for coming and let them know you're looking forward to seeing them next time.

✤ Be prepared for some women to want to hang out and talk at the end. If you need everyone to leave by a certain time, communicate this at the beginning of the group session. If you are meeting in a church during regularly scheduled activities, be aware of nursery closing times.

SESSION 1

Note: Because group members have not begun the lessons in the workbook and will only discuss the video, the format and time allotments of this session differ slightly from the others. An optional Deeper Conversation with Masterpiece Art Activity will extend the session to 90 minutes if desired.

Leader Prep

Overview

Welcome to Session 1 of *For His Glory: Living as God's Masterpiece*. Today we will discuss what it means to be God's masterpiece for His glory and watch the video for Session 1, which will prepare participants for their study in the coming week.

In Paul's succinct yet powerful Letter to the Ephesians, we find the key doctrines of the Christian faith. Ephesians helps us understand the glory of God revealed in the gospel, equips us with a clear understanding of our identity in Christ as believers, and empowers each of us to live a life worthy of our Redeemer—to live as God's masterpiece for His glory. As we study Ephesians in the coming weeks, we will ask three questions as we read the Scripture: *What does it say?, What does it mean?,* and *How does it apply to my life?*

Main Point

The Letter to the Ephesians is our how-to manual for the Christian life.

Key Scriptures

[17] I pray that the God of our Lord Jesus Christ, the Father of glory, may give you a spirit of wisdom and revelation as you come to know him, [18] so that, with the eyes of your heart enlightened, you may know what is the hope to which he has called you, what are the riches of his glorious inheritance among the saints, [19] and what is the immeasurable greatness of his power for us who believe, according to the working of his great power.

(EPHESIANS 1:17-19 NRSV)

What You Will Need

- ✣ *For His Glory* DVD and a DVD player
- ✣ Markerboard or chart paper and markers
- ✣ Stick-on name tags and markers (optional)
- ✣ iPod, smartphone, or tablet and portable speaker (optional)
- ✣ 90-minute session only: Art supplies and mini hard-backed canvases (Alternative option: card stock bookmark-sized strips)

Session Outline

Welcome and Opening Prayer (2 minutes)

To create a warm, welcoming environment as the women are gathering before the session begins, consider lighting one or more candles, providing coffee or other refreshments, and/or playing worship music. (Bring an iPod, smartphone, or tablet and a portable speaker if desired.) Be sure to provide name tags if the women do not know one another or you have new participants in your group. Then, when you are ready to begin, pray the following thematic prayer (repeating it each week), or offer your own prayer:

> *Gracious and beautiful God, thank You for the beauty that is all around us. Thank You for creating mountains and oceans and desert skies and sunsets over the ocean. With the same love, creativity, attention, and affection, You created each one of us. You call us Your masterpiece. Help us to understand what it means to live as a masterpiece, created by the Creator of the universe. Show us Your glory and teach us to live for Your glory alone. Amen.*

Icebreaker (3 minutes)

Choose one of the following questions and invite the women to share short, "popcorn" responses:

❉ When you think of the word *masterpiece*, what comes to mind first?

❉ Is there an art, craft, or home project from any season of your life, even childhood, that you remember as a "masterpiece"?

Group Discussion (20 minutes)

In the introduction, we read, "Ephesians unashamedly declares that the church is God's masterpiece—and because we are the church, that includes you and me. In Christ Jesus, we are transformed from death to life, from broken to beautiful, from rejected to chosen, from alienated to family, from defeated to victorious, from lost to redeemed. In Him we become God's masterpiece—all for the glory of His name!"

❉ How do these words resonate with you?

❉ What are you hoping to discover in these weeks of studying Ephesians together?

Video / Brief Discussion (30 minutes)

Play the Session 1 video segment on the DVD. Invite participants to complete the Session 1 Video Viewer Guide in the participant workbook as they watch (page 9).

Choose one or two questions to help you briefly share thoughts or highlights from the video:

❉ Why is the gospel good news that brings joy?

❉ How is the gospel "something that changes your status forever"?

❉ How does the phrase "from mess to masterpiece" resonate in your heart as you embark on this journey through Ephesians?

Deeper Conversation with Masterpiece Art Activity
(30 minutes, 90-minute session only)

Set out some art supplies—markers, paint pens, stickers, tissue papers, craft supplies, and so on—and a small, hard-backed canvas for each woman. Invite participants to make a simple poster of the title of the Bible study—"For His Glory"—to set on their desks at work or by the coffee maker in their kitchens or somewhere where they'll be reminded that they are a masterpiece in this world for the glory of God. (An alternative option is to provide cardstock bookmarks.) As the women create, invite them to discuss this question: *What is your response to the idea that you are God's masterpiece, created for His glory?*

Closing Prayer (5 minutes)

Close the session by taking personal prayer requests from group members and leading the group in prayer. As you progress to later weeks in the study, you might encourage members to participate in the Closing Prayer by praying out loud for one another and the requests given.

SESSION 2

Leader Prep

Overview

Welcome to Session 2 of *For His Glory: Living as God's Masterpiece*. Today we will review and discuss the lessons for Week 1 and watch the video for Session 2, which will prepare participants for their study in the coming week.

In the lessons for Week 1, we prepared the canvas by discovering the *who, what, when, where*, and most important, the *why* behind this letter to the church in Ephesus. We got to know both the author of Ephesians, the apostle Paul, and the recipients, the church in the city of Ephesus. Paul, who experienced a dramatic conversion experience when he met Jesus, was extremely devoted to this beloved church and wrote the letter as a pastor and friend.

Our readings took us all the way back to Adam and Eve, the problem of sin, and why we need a Savior. While it is true that humanity has fallen short of the glory of God and we fight against an enemy whose primary agenda is our destruction, we can rejoice that God's ultimate plan for fellowship with us was not thwarted. *The entire Epistle of Ephesians tells of the rescue mission that God initiated and completed in His Son, Jesus Christ.* God is pursuing us so that His glory can be displayed through us, His masterpiece.

Main Point

To understand the background and context of Paul's Letter to the Ephesians.

Key Scriptures

We are God's masterpiece. He has created us anew in Christ Jesus, so we can do the good things he planned for us long ago.
(EPHESIANS 2:10 NLT)

[15]"And I [Paul] said, 'Who are you, Lord?' And the Lord said, 'I am Jesus whom you are persecuting. [16]But rise and stand upon your feet, for I have appeared to you for this purpose, to appoint you as a servant and witness to the things in which you have seen me and to those in which I will appear to you, [17]delivering you from your people and from the Gentiles—to whom I am sending you [18]to open their eyes, so that they may turn from darkness to light and from the power of Satan to God, that they may receive forgiveness of sins and a place among those who are sanctified by faith in me.'"
(ACTS 26:15-18)

What You Will Need

- ✴ *For His Glory* DVD and a DVD player
- ✴ Markerboard or chart paper and markers
- ✴ Stick-on name tags and markers (optional)
- ✴ iPod, smartphone, or tablet and portable speaker (optional)

Session Outline

Welcome and Opening Prayer (2 minutes)

To create a warm, welcoming environment as the women are gathering before the session begins, consider lighting one or more candles, providing coffee or other refreshments, and/or playing worship music. (Bring an iPod, smartphone, or tablet and a portable speaker if desired.) Be sure to provide name tags if the women do not know one another or you have new participants in your group. Then, when you are ready to begin, pray the following thematic prayer (repeating it each week), or offer your own prayer:

> *Gracious and beautiful God, thank You for the beauty that is all around us. Thank You for creating mountains and oceans and desert skies and sunsets over the ocean. With the same love, creativity, attention, and affection, You created each one of us. You call us Your masterpiece. Help us to*

understand what it means to live as a masterpiece, created by the Creator of the universe. Show us Your glory and teach us to live for Your glory alone. Amen.

Icebreaker (3 minutes)

Choose one of the following questions, and invite the women to share short, "popcorn" responses:

- ✤ When you think about the "glory of God," what images come to mind?
- ✤ What is one way that your life, or the life of someone you love, showcases the glory of God?

Group Discussion (20–35 minutes, depending on session length)

Note: More material is provided than you will have time to include. Before the session, select what you want to cover, putting a check mark beside it in your book. Page references are provided for those questions that relate to specific questions or activities in the participant workbook. For these questions, invite participants to share the answers they wrote in their books. Be sure to watch your time carefully (or assign someone in the group to be the timekeeper) so that you allow enough time to watch and briefly discuss the video for Week 2 and close in prayer.

1. On page 13 in your workbook, we read, "God, the Creator of all things visible and invisible, is the ultimate artist. He has no rival or equal. He is the inventor of color and light. From His imagination came forth the brilliance of stars, the splendor of a sunrise, the majesty of mountains, and the most pivotal of His creations, you—His image bearer. Like any artist, the work of His hands reflects His glory." (Day 1)

   - ✤ What do you think it means that humans are made in God's image?
   - ✤ Look around the room at the varying hair colors, eye colors, skin tones, shapes, and sizes of the women gathered. What does that tell you about God's creativity?
   - ✤ In what ways does God's artwork point back to His character?

2. This week we looked at Adam, Eve, and the serpent in the garden. On page 15 we read, "Human beings are hardwired to live in

relationship with God. But we were not created as robots, we've been given free will, which means we can freely choose who or what we will love and worship." (Day 1)

�֍ How did Adam and Eve's choices in the garden shape the human experience?

✤ How have you personally tasted of the destruction of sin and the devastation it brings to God's image bearers? (page 17)

✤ What does the fact that we have free will tell us about God?

3. On page 19 we read, "Glory is God's *why*! He orchestrated a divine plan to restore a lost humanity to Himself for one magnificent reason— to showcase His glory to the world. It is through this rescue mission, which we call the gospel, that God's heart is most clearly revealed. Through redemption, love is defined. Through the gospel, we discover a Father who pursues us in order to reconcile us." (Day 2)

✤ When have you felt pursued by God?

✤ How would you tell the good news of the gospel—redemption and love—in your own words?

✤ What have you learned about the heart of God in your readings this week?

4. Three important words in Ephesians are *grace*, *truth*, and *redemption*. On page 23 we read, "As we look at Jesus, we see God is full of grace and truth. This means that He is for you and not against you. This means that God is pursuing you so that His glory can be displayed through you, His masterpiece." (Day 2)

✤ What did you learn about the words *grace*, *truth*, and *redemption* in Day 2? What resonated in your heart as you read about those special and spiritual words?

✤ What does God's renovation work in your own life look like right now: imagining a new design; demolition; rebuilding; designing; or the big reveal?

5. Reflect together on these words: "What I've come to understand after nearly two decades of this redeemed life is this: **Jesus didn't just save me *from* my sins; Jesus freed me *for* the incredible life my heavenly Father destined for me**." (Day 3)

    ✤ How have you been saved sin and also saved *for* a life with God?

    ✤ What does it look like to live the "redeemed life"?

6. The apostle Paul's conversion story is a demonstration that God can soften and change even the hardest of hearts. God can do a renovation in us, no matter how far from God we feel. (Day 3)

    ✤ Read aloud Acts 9:1-22. How did Paul's conversion story speak to you?

    ✤ How did Paul describe his life before he met Jesus on the road to Damascus? (page 29)

    ✤ If you're comfortable sharing, tell about your own conversion story. How did the light of God break through in a way that revealed your desperation for God?

7. Paul preached in Ephesus for two years with immense response to his message. On page 34 we read, "As a result of Paul's teaching, those who believed experienced genuine life change, just as Jesus told Paul they would—they turned from darkness to light." (Day 4)

    ✤ Look back at your notes on pages 33–34 (following "To better understand Paul's ministry in Ephesus . . ."). What is Paul's relationship with the city of Ephesus?

    ✤ How would you describe Paul's relationship with the church in Ephesus? How does that depth of affection give context to his Letter to the Ephesians?

    ✤ What did Paul say he taught the people in Ephesus? (page 35)

8. After our conversion experience, we get to tell others about the good news we've discovered in Jesus Christ. On page 37 we read, "Jesus' plan to transform the world and rescue humanity involved a simple strategy: discipleship. Discipleship is the act of one person teaching another how to know God personally and walk in His truth." (Day 5)

    ✷ What is your understanding of the word *discipleship*? How is discipleship Jesus' plan to transform the world?

    ✷ What are some examples of discipleship happening in your church and community?

    ✷ Who has God used to help grow and establish your faith in Jesus? Who has been like the apostle Paul in your spiritual journey, and how has this person impacted your life? (page 37)

9. As we continue in Ephesians, we'll see that Paul wrote to the church out of deep love for them and to protect them from false teachers. On page 39 we read, "Paul knew young believers would be easy prey for false teachers. He feared the 'savage wolves' would ravage the flock. So Paul wrote to remind the flock of the essential truths of the Christian faith so that the false teachers could not distort it and divide the church." (Day 5)

    ✷ Read 1 Timothy 1:3-7, where Paul warns Timothy about those "savage wolves" who are trying to distort the truth by teaching a different doctrine. What do you think Paul is concerned will happen to his beloved church in Ephesus? (page 39)

    ✷ What are some modern examples of false teachers distorting the gospel and dividing the church?

    ✷ What does this passage tell us about Paul's heart for the church?

10. Think about all of your study and reflection this week.

    ✷ What thoughts or discoveries are sticking with you from this week's study?

Deeper Conversation (10 minutes)

Divide into smaller groups of two or three for deeper conversation. (Encourage the women to break into different groups each week.) Before the session, write on a markerboard or chart paper the following question:

✤ Paul's personal mission statement from Philippians 1:21 says, ". . . To live is Christ, and to die is gain." Share about your life purpose—what fuels your life and gives meaning to your day? (page 38)

Give a two-minute warning before time is up so that the groups may wrap up their discussion.

Video / Brief Discussion (30–35 minutes, depending on session length)

Play the Session 2 video segment on the DVD. Invite participants to complete the Video Viewer Guide for Session 2 in the participant workbook as they watch (page 41).

Afterward, choose one or two questions to help you briefly share thoughts or highlights from the video:

✤ What are some ways we can define the word *hope*?

✤ What does it mean to be "in Christ"?

✤ How do we showcase God's glory to the world?

Closing Prayer (5 minutes)

Close the session by taking personal prayer requests from group members and leading the group in prayer. As you progress to later weeks in the study, you might encourage members to participate in the Closing Prayer by praying out loud for one another and the requests given.

SESSION 3

Leader Prep

Overview

Welcome to Session 3 of *For His Glory: Living as God's Masterpiece*. Today we will review and discuss the lessons for Week 2 and watch the video for Session 3, which will prepare participants for their study in the coming week.

In the lessons for Week 2, we dove into Ephesians to see that this letter begins with rapturous praise to God the Father for the brilliance, majesty, and perfection of His design to save us and to adopt us into His very own family. Paul then shifts his gaze to behold the love of Jesus, who sacrificially died to redeem us; and then Paul praises the Holy Spirit who is the sign and seal of our inheritance.

We explored what it means that God is a good Father who looks on us with eyes of affection and who, out of love, paid the price of redemption for us. Because of Jesus' sacrifice for us, we have a spiritual inheritance as heirs in God's kingdom. We have the promise of a future with God and a promise of the presence of God with us right now through the Holy Spirit.

Main Point

To discover the glory of the gospel.

Key Scripture

[2]Grace to you and peace from God our Father and the Lord Jesus Christ. [3]Blessed be the God and Father of our Lord Jesus Christ, who has blessed us in Christ with every spiritual blessing in the heavenly places, [4]even as he chose us in him before the foundation of the world, that we should be holy and blameless before him. In love [5]he predestined us for adoption to himself as sons through Jesus Christ, according to the purpose of his will, [6]to the praise of his glorious grace, with which he has blessed us in the Beloved.

(EPHESIANS 1:2-6)

What You Will Need

- ❄ *For His Glory* DVD and a DVD player
- ❄ Markerboard or chart paper and markers
- ❄ Stick-on name tags and markers (optional)
- ❄ iPod, smartphone, or tablet and portable speaker (optional)

Session Outline

Welcome and Opening Prayer (2 minutes)

To create a warm, welcoming environment as the women are gathering before the session begins, consider lighting one or more candles, providing coffee or other refreshments, and/or playing worship music. (Bring an iPod, smartphone, or tablet and a portable speaker if desired.) Be sure to provide name tags if the women do not know one another or you have new participants in your group. Then, when you are ready to begin, pray the following thematic prayer (repeating it each week), or offer your own prayer:

> *Gracious and beautiful God, thank You for the beauty that is all around us. Thank You for creating mountains and oceans and desert skies and sunsets over the ocean. With the same love, creativity, attention, and affection, You created each one of us. You call us Your masterpiece. Help us to understand what it means to live as a masterpiece, created by the Creator of the universe. Show us Your glory and teach us to live for Your glory alone. Amen.*

Icebreaker (3 minutes)

Choose one of the following questions and invite the women to share short, "popcorn" responses:

- ❄ What is the most beautiful piece of artwork you have ever seen? What about that particular artwork drew/draws you to it?
- ❄ What is one metaphor or illustration that has helped you understand the Trinity—the relationship between God the Father, Jesus Christ the Son, and the Holy Spirit?

Group Discussion (20–35 minutes, depending on session length)

Note: More material is provided than you will have time to include. Before the session, select what you want to cover, putting a check mark beside it in your book. Page references are provided for those questions that relate to specific questions or activities in the participant workbook. For these questions, invite participants to share the answers they wrote in their books. Be sure to watch your time carefully (or assign someone in the group to be the timekeeper) so that you allow enough time to watch and briefly discuss the video for Week 3 and close in prayer.

1. Our last two sessions have set the stage for the content of Paul's Letter to the Ephesians. Read aloud Ephesians 1:3-6. (Day 1)

   ✣ Who is Paul writing in praise of? Why is Paul praising God?

   ✣ What did you discover about spiritual blessings?

   ✣ How do we receive the spiritual blessings?

2. In our lessons this week, we were invited to ponder this thought: "Before God spoke the universe into existence, He saw you. He loved you. He chose you. If you're anything like me, you may have struggled with feelings of rejection your whole life, but let me assure you of one thing—you were never rejected by God!" (Day 1)

   ✣ Read aloud Ephesians 1:4 again. When did God the Father choose you to be His own? (page 45)

   ✣ If we are "in Christ," how are we seen in the eyes of God the Father? (page 45)

   ✣ How does the truth that being in Christ means God sees you as "holy and without fault" strike your heart today? (page 45)

3. Moving from the deep love and affection of God the Father, let's discuss the work of Jesus in our lives. On pages 51–52 we read, "Jesus taught that sin isn't just something we have (like a cold virus); sin is something that has us. It is something that holds us in captivity, refusing to let us go. We don't have control over it; it has control over us. The picture is a slave controlled by a master. Sin holds us captive and refuses to let us go unless a ransom is paid, which is precisely what God did to solve our problem." (Day 2)

    ✤   Is there anything in your life you've felt powerless against? A sinful habit you couldn't break or a temptation you couldn't resist? Describe how it makes you feel. (page 51)

    ✤   Read John 8:34-36. What did Jesus say the Son of God is able to do? (page 51)

    ✤   Read Romans 3:23-25. Ask volunteers to retell these verses in their own words.

4.   Read the definition of atonement from page 53—"**Atonement**: The word *atonement* means to 'cover over.' The sacrificial lamb served as a substitute. Instead of a man or woman dying for his or her sins, God provided the lamb to take the place of that person, and the blood of the lamb paid the penalty for their sin—covering over their sin." (Day 2)

    ✤   What did you learn about atonement in your readings? What questions do you still have about it?

    ✤   How does understanding the significance of the sacrificial lamb help you appreciate the forgiveness and freedom Jesus lavished upon you? (page 55)

    ✤   How does seeing the price Jesus paid to redeem you change how you see yourself? (page 55)

5.   In Christ, we receive spiritual blessings and have access to God's immeasurable riches. Review the "I am" statements on page 58. (Day 3)

    ✤   What is the spiritual inheritance or the spiritual blessings we see in Ephesians 1–2?

    ✤   How might these spiritual blessings change the way we live our daily lives?

    ✤   How have you experienced these blessings in your own life— forgiveness, acceptance, love, freedom, victory?

6. This week we learned that, biblically speaking, our inheritance is our full salvation, which will be completed upon Jesus' return. On page 59 we read, "Inheritance has a present tense reality and holds a future tense promise. Presently, we are set free from the domain of darkness, and our future hope is full restoration with God in heaven." (Day 3)

   ❈ Our spiritual inheritance points to the eternal future we have with Christ. How does the truth and hope of this future give you confidence and joy in the midst of hard circumstances? (page 60)

   ❈ How does it make you feel to be called a child of God—an heir in the kingdom of God?

7. Read aloud Ephesians 1:13. Paul declares that whoever trusts in Jesus as Savior receives the Holy Spirit. On page 62 we read, "There isn't a special club or group of Christians who receive the Spirit; actually, the evidence that someone is a Christian is the fact that the Holy Spirit is in his or her life." (Day 4)

   ❈ What did you learn this week about the purpose of the Holy Spirit? (refer to page 63)

   ❈ In what ways have you seen evidence of the Holy Spirit working in your life? (page 64)

   ❈ What is an example of the visible work of the Holy Spirit in someone else's life?

8. Search online for the lyrics to the chorus of the old hymn "Victory in Jesus" or a contemporary praise song about our victory through Jesus' death on the cross, and read the words aloud (or, if you prefer, play or sing the song together). (Day 5)

   ❈ How have you known victory in Jesus?

   ❈ How does Jesus bring our victory over defeat and despair?

   ❈ What does it mean to say that "victory is our inheritance"?

9. God's Word reveals that the key to victory is simply to acknowledge our weakness and confess our dependence upon Jesus. This requires humility and faith. In humility we confess our need for God, and in faith we acknowledge that only God can give us the strength to do what is impossible for us apart from Him. (Day 5)

    ✸ Read Ephesians 1:15-19. How would you restate those verses in your own words?

    ✸ Would you say that you depend more on God or on your own strength? Why?

    ✸ How can you rely more on God to supply your needs?

10. Think about all of your study and reflection this week.

    ✸ What thoughts or discoveries are sticking with you from this week's study?

Deeper Conversation (10 minutes)

Divide into smaller groups of two or three for deeper conversation. (Encourage the women to break into different groups each week.) Before the session, write on a markerboard or chart paper the follow question:

    ✸ Read 2 Corinthians 12:9 together. Where do you feel weak and in need of God's power today? (page 72) When and how have you experienced God's strength in your weakness?

Give a two-minute warning before time is up so that the groups may wrap up their discussion.

Video / Brief Discussion (30–35 minutes, depending on session length)

Play the Session 3 video segment on the DVD. Invite participants to complete the Video Viewer Guide for Session 3 in the participant workbook as they watch (page 74).

Choose one or two questions to help you *briefly* discuss thoughts or highlights from the video:

* ✳ What did you hear about your identity in Christ?

* ✳ Do you ever struggle from having a wrong identity? What does that look like for you?

* ✳ How are we able to listen to the Voice of Truth?

Closing Prayer (5 minutes)

Close the session by taking personal prayer requests from group members and leading the group in prayer. As you progress to later weeks in the study, you might encourage members to participate in the Closing Prayer by praying out loud for one another and the requests given.

SESSION 4

Leader Prep

Overview

Welcome to Session 4 of *For His Glory: Living as God's Masterpiece*. Today we will review and discuss the lessons for Week 3 and watch the video for Session 4, which will prepare participants for their study in the coming week.

In the lessons for Week 3, we moved into Ephesians 2 and 3 to learn about the gift of salvation from the perspective of the individual who is redeemed. We discovered who we were before God rescued us, what God did for us in delivering us from the domain of darkness, and who we are as the result of that divine deliverance. Each lesson emphasized a new element of our identity in Christ—we are saved by grace; we are His masterpiece; we are the temple of the Holy Spirit; we are the church; and we are lavishly loved.

Main Point

To discover who we were before God rescued us, what God did for us in delivering us from the domain of darkness, and who we are as the result of that divine deliverance.

Key Scriptures

¹You were dead in the trespasses and sins ²in which you once walked, following the course of this world, following the prince of the power of the air, the spirit that is now at work in the sons of disobedience— ³among whom we all once lived in the passions of our flesh, carrying out the desires of the body and the mind, and were by nature children of wrath, like the rest of mankind. ⁴But God, being rich in mercy, because of the great love with which he loved us, ⁵even when we were dead in our trespasses, made us alive together with Christ—by grace you have been saved— ⁶and raised us up with him and seated us with him in the heavenly places in Christ Jesus, ⁷so that in the

coming ages he might show the immeasurable riches of his
grace in kindness toward us in Christ Jesus.
(EPHESIANS 2:1-7)

[8]*God saved you by his grace when you believed. And you*
can't take credit for this; it is a gift from God. [9]*Salvation is not*
a reward for the good things we have done, so none of us can
boast about it. [10]*For we are God's masterpiece. He has created*
us anew in Christ Jesus, so we can do the good things he
planned for us long ago.
(EPHESIANS 2:8-10 NLT)

What You Will Need

✢   *For His Glory* DVD and a DVD player

✢   Markerboard or chart paper and markers

✢   Stick-on name tags and markers (optional)

✢   iPod, smartphone, or tablet and portable speaker (optional)

Session Outline

Welcome and Opening Prayer (2 minutes)

To create a warm, welcoming environment as the women are gathering
before the session begins, consider lighting one or more candles, providing
coffee or other refreshments, and/or playing worship music. (Bring an
iPod, smartphone, or tablet and a portable speaker if desired.) Be sure to
provide name tags if the women do not know one another or you have new
participants in your group. Then, when you are ready to begin, pray the
following thematic prayer (repeating it each week), or offer your own prayer:

> *Gracious and beautiful God, thank You for the beauty that is*
> *all around us. Thank You for creating mountains and oceans*
> *and desert skies and sunsets over the ocean. With the*
> *same love, creativity, attention, and affection, You created*
> *each one of us. You call us Your masterpiece. Help us to*

understand what it means to live as a masterpiece, created by the Creator of the universe. Show us Your glory and teach us to live for Your glory alone. Amen.

Icebreaker (3 minutes)
Invite the women to share short, "popcorn" responses to the following prompt:

- This week we are studying what it means to be rescued by God. Share briefly a time when you were rescued in some way.

Group Discussion (20–35 minutes, depending on session length)
Note: More material is provided than you will have time to include. Before the session, select what you want to cover, putting a check mark beside it in your book. Page references are provided for those questions that relate to specific questions or activities in the participant workbook. For these questions, invite participants to share the answers they wrote in their books. Be sure to watch your time carefully (or assign someone in the group to be the timekeeper) so that you allow enough time to watch and briefly discuss the video for Week 4 and close in prayer.

1. On page 77 we read, "If [Ephesians 2:1-7] were an extreme makeover show, we would call these verses our 'before and after pictures.' First we see the bleakest terms possible to describe the human condition apart from God's saving grace (our before picture), and then we learn of our new status in Christ (our after picture)." (Day 1)

    - Read Ephesians 2:1-7 aloud. How does your heart respond to these verses? (page 77)
    - What is the desperate state of humanity in verse 1? (page 77)
    - Read Colossians 1:12-13 aloud. Why did God rescue us? Why did He set us free from the dominion of darkness?

2. On page 80 we read, "Ephesians can be summed up in three simple words: *sit, walk, stand*. First we are 'seated with Christ' in His victory (chapters 1–2). Next we learn to 'walk' in this world as God's masterpieces (chapters 3–5). Finally, we learn to 'stand' against the spiritual forces that

oppose us (chapter 6). From beginning to end, the Christian life is about relying on what Jesus Christ accomplished for us on the cross and then appropriating this truth into our daily lives." (Day 1)

✢ How would you explain what it means to be "seated with Christ"? (page 80)

✢ How does being "seated with Christ" illustrate the gift of grace? (page 80)

✢ Read Matthew 11:28-30 aloud. What does Jesus offer the weary? (page 81)

3. This week we considered that we owe everything to God's grace. It is God who redeemed us, and we can't take any credit for it. (Day 2)

✢ From what you've learned so far about God's mercy and grace, why would boasting be out of the question? (page 84)

✢ What are some ways that we as human beings try to earn God's favor or work our way into His family? (page 84)

✢ What is something you've been tempted to "boast in" or to believe it makes you more loved by God? (page 84)

4. On page 85 we read, "We respond to God's love with love for our neighbor. We respond to God's mercy with mercy for others. We reflect the glory of God to the world by showcasing His transforming power in our lives." (Day 2)

✢ What does it look like to live your life in response to the grace of God?

✢ How do our transformed lives display the glory of God?

✢ Would you say that your relationship with God is marked by duty or delight? Do you feel yourself striving to earn His favor or responding to His lavish grace? (page 86)

5. "As Christ's followers, *we* are now the temple of God's Holy Spirit." (Day 3)

   ✤ Read Ephesians 2:11-21 aloud. Review your notes from Day 3. What would have been radical about these words for the first audience of Paul's letter?

   ✤ How does Jesus bring groups together?

   ✤ What does it mean to be the temple of God's Holy Spirit?

6. On pages 92–93 we read, "God desires to dwell with us. What was lost in the garden of Eden, He restores. He is the initiator of relationship and has created a way for us to be in His presence. The Old Testament Tabernacle and temple and all of the sacrifices performed there all pointed forward to Jesus Christ who perfectly fulfilled each symbol and sacrifice and who is the ultimate way that we can access the presence of God." (Day 3)

   ✤ Read Exodus 25:8. What was God's desire? (page 92)

   ✤ What does it mean to you that God is the initiator of relationship?

   ✤ Given that Scripture declares a Christian is the temple of God's Spirit, where His glory dwells, what implications does this truth hold for your daily life? (page 94)

7. This week we were reminded that the church is not a building or a program but a people. On page 97 we read, "Through the church, God displays His glory, wisdom, and divine plan. It is vital for you and me to understand that we are members of God's body and that, as His church, it is through us that He works out His plan for the world." (Day 4)

   ✤ What do you think of when you hear the word *church*?

   ✤ Read Ephesians 3:10. What is God's goal for the church? (page 96)

   ✤ How does this insight change or challenge your view of the church? (page 97)

8. Recall the analogy of us "dating" the church. As we read on pages **97–98**, sometimes we can "hop from one service to another, taking

good teaching from one place and incredible worship from another, without committing ourselves to love, give, and serve alongside a community of believers. Many of us approach the church from a consumer mentality instead of a commitment one." (Day 4)

- What do you think about the analogy of us "dating the church"?
- True confessions: Have you ever dated the church? Share about what you were looking for or missing in some churches.
- How does a consumer mentality keep us from actually being the church?

9. These words from page 100 capture the struggle many of us have in believing that God loves us: "Although I loved Jesus passionately, something was missing. I was still a little girl performing to earn her daddy's love—believing the lie I must be perfect to deserve it. You see, I knew of God's love on an intellectual level, but my heart had not apprehended it." (Day 5)

    - Can you relate? Do you ever feel numb to the fact that God loves you? (page 101)
    - Read Romans 8:15. How does Paul tell us that we can come to God?
    - What are some ways we can believe God's love for us more fully?

10. This week we were reminded that there is no limit to what God can do for us, and He can do "infinitely more" than we can ask or imagine. On page 106 we read, "One of my favorite expressions I like to use for my own encouragement is 'He's got this.' I'm a simple woman of faith; my vocabulary is no match for the great apostle Paul's. What this short phrase does for my heart is remind me that there is nothing my God can't provide, accomplish, heal, or restore." (Day 5)

    - How do fears and unbelief hinder our prayers?
    - Do you have any short phrases that remind you to trust God?
    - Read Ephesians 3:16-19 aloud. What results when we grasp the love of God "that surpasses knowledge"? What are we filled with? (page 105)

11. Think about all of your study and reflection this week.

  ✻ What thoughts or discoveries are sticking with you from this week's study?

Deeper Conversation (10 minutes)

Divide into smaller groups of two or three for deeper conversation. (Encourage the women to break into different groups each week.) Before the session, write on a markerboard or chart paper the question or questions you want the groups to discuss:

  ✻ What are some ways we can deepen our intimacy with God and experience more of His love?

  ✻ What transforming work do you need God to do in your life?

Give a two-minute warning before time is up so that the groups may wrap up their discussion.

Video / Brief Discussion (30–35 minutes, depending on session length)

Play the Session 4 video segment on the DVD. Invite participants to complete the Video Viewer Guide for Session 4 in the participant workbook as they watch (page 107).

Choose one or two questions to help you briefly share thoughts or highlights from the video:

  ✻ What does it mean to walk worthy?

  ✻ What did you hear in the video that stuck out to you or challenged you?

Closing Prayer (5 minutes)

Close the session by taking personal prayer requests from group members and leading the group in prayer. As you progress to later weeks in the study, you might encourage members to participate in the Closing Prayer by praying out loud for one another and the requests given.

SESSION 5

Leader Prep

Overview

Welcome to Session 5 of *For His Glory: Living as God's Masterpiece*. Today we will review and discuss the lessons for Week 4 and watch the video for Session 5, which will prepare participants for their study in the coming week.

The lessons for Week 4 brought us to the middle of Ephesians where Paul begins to teach us to walk in a manner worthy of our calling—in other words, to align our belief and our behavior. We searched the Scriptures for instruction about living in community, living in the Spirit, and letting the Spirit work in us to change our behavior from the inside out.

Main Point

To learn what it means to walk worthy of the grace that redeems us.

Key Scriptures

¹Therefore I, the prisoner of the Lord, implore you to walk in a manner worthy of the calling with which you have been called, ²with all humility and gentleness, with patience, showing tolerance for one another in love, ³being diligent to preserve the unity of the Spirit in the bond of peace. ⁴There is one body and one Spirit, just as also you were called in one hope of your calling; ⁵one Lord, one faith, one baptism, ⁶one God and Father of all who is over all and through all and in all.

(EPHESIANS 4:1-6 NASB)

¹⁴Then we will no longer be infants, tossed back and forth by the waves, and blown here and there by every wind of teaching and by the cunning and craftiness of people in their deceitful scheming. ¹⁵Instead, speaking the truth in love, we will grow to become in every respect the mature body of him who is the

head, that is, Christ. [16]*From him the whole body, joined and held together by every supporting ligament, grows and builds itself up in love, as each part does its work.*
(*EPHESIANS 4:14-16 NIV*)

What You Will Need

- ❖ *For His Glory* DVD and a DVD player
- ❖ Markerboard or chart paper and markers
- ❖ Stick-on name tags and markers (optional)
- ❖ iPod, smartphone, or tablet and portable speaker (optional)

Session Outline

Welcome and Opening Prayer (2 minutes)

To create a warm, welcoming environment as the women are gathering before the session begins, consider lighting one or more candles, providing coffee or other refreshments, and/or playing worship music. (Bring an iPod, smartphone, or tablet and a portable speaker if desired.) Be sure to provide name tags if the women do not know one another or you have new participants in your group. Then, when you are ready to begin, pray the following thematic prayer (repeating it each week), or offer your own prayer:

> *Gracious and beautiful God, thank You for the beauty that is all around us. Thank You for creating mountains and oceans and desert skies and sunsets over the ocean. With the same love, creativity, attention, and affection, You created each one of us. You call us Your masterpiece. Help us to understand what it means to live as a masterpiece, created by the Creator of the universe. Show us Your glory and teach us to live for Your glory alone. Amen.*

Icebreaker (3 minutes)

Invite the women to share short, "popcorn" responses to the following question:

✢ What are the many "hats" you wear right now? Describe how you might behave in each hat. For example, your soccer mom hat might mean that you gear up in your sunscreen and hat, fill the cooler with drinks and snacks, load the van with folding chairs, and go cheer for the team.

Group Discussion (20–35 minutes, depending on session length)
Note: More material is provided than you will have time to include. Before the session, select what you want to cover, putting a check mark beside it in your book. Page references are provided for those questions that relate to specific questions or activities in the participant workbook. For these questions, invite participants to share the answers they wrote in their books. Be sure to watch your time carefully (or assign someone in the group to be the timekeeper) so that you allow enough time to watch and briefly discuss the video for Week 5 and close in prayer.

1. On page 110 we read, "In Ephesians, we are called to give equal weight to our beliefs and our behavior. It is not okay for us to claim to be Christians and not reflect our beliefs in our behavior. Today, we call this hypocritical behavior, but the Bible calls it living in a manner unworthy of our calling." (Day 1)

   ✢ What are some examples of hypocritical behaviors?
   ✢ Do you find it difficult to live out your calling as a follower of Christ?
   ✢ Read Ephesians 4:1-6 aloud. How would you put this passage into your own words?

2. "Each of these attributes—humility, gentleness, patience, and tolerance—enables us to maintain unity within the church." (Day 1)

   ✢ What did you discover in your Scripture study about each of these words—humility, gentleness, patience, tolerance? Refer to pages 111–13 in your workbook.
   ✢ Would you say you are quick to demonstrate these characteristics, or do you find them difficult? Explain your response.
   ✢ Why are these things important for the work of unity in the church and in the world?

3. On pages 117–18 we read, "The apostle Paul declares to those of us who are in Christ that our lives are meant to be lived on mission. This calling echoes Jesus' words in the Great Commission when He told the disciples to 'go and make disciples of all nations' (Matthew 28:19 NIV). Jesus made our calling crystal clear: to tell the world about Him and to teach others how to be His disciples. Though each of us will fulfill this calling in different ways using different gifts, we share the same purpose." (Day 2)

   - Read Ephesians 4:7-13. What is the purpose of these gifts? (page 118)
   - What is the result of each person using her or his spiritual gift? What is accomplished in the church? (page 118)
   - Where do these spiritual gifts come from? Recall a time when you tried to live out the gifts in your own strength, and tell about that time.

4. This week we learned that spiritual gifts aren't discovered through quizzes but through serving and obeying God, using what is in our hand. On page 120 we read, "The Lord told Moses that he would use that staff in his hand and through it perform miracles, miracles that would deliver His people and show His redeeming love. All God needed was what was in Moses' hand. Moses would now shepherd God's people out of slavery in Egypt." (Day 2)

   - Read Exodus 3:10; 4:1-2. Why did God want to know what was in Moses' hand? What do you think that means for us?
   - What has the Lord placed in your hand [that He can use for His glory]? (page 121)
   - Has God ever used you in the making of a miracle? If so, tell about that time.

5. Paul instructs us to seek spiritual maturity. On page 124 we read, "Spiritual growth is the expectation we find in Scripture. In God's plan, the new life of Christ that is created in us at our salvation is meant to flourish and mature. Just as an infant is nourished and grows into a toddler, then into a child, and then into a teenager who, thankfully, becomes an adult, so too a child of God also matures." (Day 3)

✤ What does spiritual maturity look like in the life of a Jesus-follower? (Refer to the qualities of a maturing child of God that you listed on page 125.)

✤ What does spiritual immaturity look like?

✤ Where would you say you are on the spectrum of spiritual newborn to a spiritual elder? How is God currently maturing you? (page 125) What have you learned that can help you grow in spiritual maturity?

6. We can't will ourselves to mature on our own effort; it's the Holy Spirit who helps us to grow in Christ. On page 127 we read, "Jesus called the Holy Spirit our 'Helper.' He is the one who comes alongside us and helps us in our weaknesses. The Spirit transforms us from the inside out to act, to think, and to love like Jesus. As we see an area in which we need to mature, we ask the Holy Spirit to take the lead and do the work of transformation." (Day 3)

✤ How have you experienced the work of the Holy Spirit in your own life to bring about a new level of spiritual maturity?

✤ Read John 14:26 aloud. What does this verse tell you about the role of the Holy Spirit?

✤ What does it mean that the Holy Spirit comes alongside you to teach you and remind you everything Jesus has taught you? How has this been true in your own life?

7. "As a Christ-follower, who has been redeemed from sin and darkness, our call is to no longer walk in that old lifestyle. I'm not saying we will never sin or be tempted by it, but our lifestyle should be one that increasingly reflects God's holiness, love, and goodness. Our walk should reveal the transformation that has occurred in our hearts because of the gospel." (Day 4)

✤ Read Ephesians 4:17-24 and John 8:12 aloud. What do these verses teach us about how we walk as Christ-followers? (Refer to pages 129–30.)

✸ What are some things that you do to stay close to God and help you to walk in a way that reveals God's work in your life?

8. On page 133 we read, "Our 'old self' was once enslaved to the world's way of selfish thinking, and our hearts were once hard toward God because of sin. But now as Christ-followers, we live for the glory of God." (Day 4)

   ✸ What is something you've chased after, hoping it would fulfill you, that only resulted in more emptiness? (page 132)

   ✸ How would you compare and contrast your life before and after following Christ?

   ✸ How would you tell someone about the new life available in Jesus?

9. On page 136, we read that the new self is "100 percent righteous. . . . Because Jesus is pure holiness and we are 'in Him.' Grasping this truth is fundamental to our walk. We aren't striving to become more holy; we are laying aside our old self to walk in our new nature." (Day 5)

   ✸ How do these words encourage you today?

   ✸ Have you ever found yourself striving to become more holy? How did that go?

   ✸ How would you explain or describe your identity in Christ? How can you live out of that identity instead of all the other things that try to tell you who you are?

10. Paul teaches us to take off some things that keep us trapped in our old life and to put on some things that help us to display God's glory. (Day 5)

    ✸ Read Ephesians 4:25-32 aloud. What does Paul instruct us to take off? (Refer to page 136.) What does it mean to take off things such as falsehood and anger?

    ✸ How difficult is it to lay aside our old ways? Share an example from your own life if you are willing.

11. Think about all of your study and reflection this week.

  ✤ What thoughts or discoveries are sticking with you from this
     week's study?

Deeper Conversation (10 minutes)
Divide into smaller groups of two or three for deeper conversation.
(Encourage the women to break into different groups each week.) Before
the session, write on a markerboard or chart paper the question you want
the groups to discuss:

  ✤ Have you ever felt the Holy Spirit calling you to lay aside an old
     sinful practice? (page 138) How has the Spirit been working in you
     to lay that aside?

Give a two-minute warning before time is up so that the groups may wrap
up their discussion.

Video / Brief Discussion (30–35 minutes)
Play the Session 5 video segment on the DVD. Invite participants to
complete the Video Viewer Guide for Session 5 in the participant workbook
as they watch (page 142).
  Choose one or two questions to help you briefly share thoughts or
highlights from the video:

  ✤ What did you hear about living in the light of God?

  ✤ How do we live in the light?

Closing Prayer (5 minutes)
Close the session by taking personal prayer requests from group members
and leading the group in prayer. Invite members to participate in the
Closing Prayer by praying out loud for one another and the requests given.

SESSION 6

Leader Prep

Overview

Welcome to Session 6 of *For His Glory: Living as God's Masterpiece*. Today we will review and discuss the lessons for Week 5 and watch the video for Week 6, which will prepare participants for their study in the coming week.

In the lessons for Week 5 we read about what it means to live in the light of God. We learned what it means to be imitators of Christ and to be filled with the Spirit as we learn to live for His glory. Ephesians shines the light of Christ into our relationships, our marriages, and even our control issues. Imitating Christ means yielding to His will, His instruction, and His glory.

Main Point

To learn how to shine a spotlight on Jesus with our lives.

Key Scriptures

¹*Be imitators of God, as beloved children.* ²*And walk in love, as Christ loved us and gave himself up for us, a fragrant offering and sacrifice to God.*
(EPHESIANS 5:1-2)

⁸*At one time you were darkness, but now you are light in the Lord. Walk as children of light* ⁹*(for the fruit of light is found in all that is good and right and true),* ¹⁰*and try to discern what is pleasing to the Lord.*
(EPHESIANS 5:8-10)

What You Will Need

✳ *For His Glory* DVD and a DVD player

✳ Markerboard or chart paper and markers

✳ Stick-on name tags and markers (optional)

✳ iPod, smartphone, or tablet and portable speaker (optional)

Session Outline

Welcome and Opening Prayer (2 minutes)

To create a warm, welcoming environment as the women are gathering before the session begins, consider lighting one or more candles, providing coffee or other refreshments, and/or playing worship music. (Bring an iPod, smartphone, or tablet and a portable speaker if desired.) Be sure to provide name tags if the women do not know one another or you have new participants in your group. Then, when you are ready to begin, pray the following thematic prayer (repeating it each week), or offer your own prayer:

> Gracious and beautiful God, thank You for the beauty that is all around us. Thank You for creating mountains and oceans and desert skies and sunsets over the ocean. With the same love, creativity, attention, and affection, You created each one of us. You call us Your masterpiece. Help us to understand what it means to live as a masterpiece, created by the Creator of the universe. Show us Your glory and teach us to live for Your glory alone. Amen.

Icebreaker (3 minutes)

Invite the women to share short, "popcorn" responses to the following question:

* If you could imitate or be like anyone *in the world*, who would it be? Why him or her?

Group Discussion (20–35 minutes, depending on session length)

Note: More material is provided than you will have time to include. Before the session, select what you want to cover, putting a check mark beside it in your book. Page references are provided for those questions that relate to specific questions or activities in the participant workbook. For these questions, invite participants to share the answers they wrote in their books. Be sure to watch your time carefully (or assign someone in the group to be the timekeeper) so that you allow enough time to watch and briefly discuss the video for Week 6 and close in prayer.

1. As Christians, the reason for our changed behavior is a changed identity. On page 146 we read, "We don't love others in order to earn favor with God; we love others because He first loved us. All Christian ethics spring from a Christ-centered identity. Because I am the 'beloved' I am called to walk in love." (Day 1)

   ✣ Read Matthew 5:43-48. Why does Jesus call us to love our neighbor? (page 146)

   ✣ How does the idea that "because I am the 'beloved' I am called to walk in love" resonate with you? Share your thoughts in response to this statement.

   ✣ Do you see your identity as one who is loved by God? Why or why not?

2. On page 147 we read this confession and reflection: "There are people in my life I'm called to love whom I don't even like sometimes. But my feelings have nothing to do with my obedience to God's call. I am called to love others with the same lavish love extended to me by God." (Day 1)

   ✣ Can you relate to the struggle of being called to love people you don't even like? Share your thoughts and feelings briefly.

   ✣ Read John 15:1-14 aloud. What does Jesus promise, and what is the result of abiding? (page 148)

   ✣ Read Galatians 5:22-23 aloud. What is produced in the life of a branch connected to the Vine? (page 149)

   ✣ What are some ways that we can walk in love, even when we don't feel love toward certain people?

3. This week we acknowledged a tension we all face as Christ-followers: "We are called the 'light of world,' yet we live in the midst of darkness that seeks to conform us to its agenda." (Day 2)

   ✣ In what ways have you felt the tension of a darkness that seeks to conform us to its agenda?

✳ Read Romans 12:2 aloud. What does this verse say about the pressure to conform? (page 154) How does this make it difficult to live in the light?

✳ Have you known life with God to be better than any temporary pleasure sin could offer? Elaborate on your response.

4. Reflect on the idea that whatever fills us, controls us. On page 161 we read, "The person filled with alcohol is controlled by alcohol. The person filled with anger is controlled by anger. The same proves true for lust, greed, and envy. The good news is that this principle also proves true of Jesus. When His Spirit fills us, our thoughts, words, actions, and reactions are under His control. Or rather, they are 'under the influence' of God." (Day 3)

✳ When have you experienced being filled and controlled by something (an emotion, a substance, or a thought)? (page 161)

✳ How does being under the influence of the Holy Spirit change or alter our behavior, thoughts, and feelings?

✳ How does this concept help you understand what it means to walk worthy?

5. "If we are filled with the Holy Spirit, the proof pours forth in praise." (Day 3)

✳ What do you think this statement means?

✳ Read Ephesians 5:18b-20. According to this verse, what does it mean to be filled with the Holy Spirit?

✳ What do you think it means to make music to the Lord in your heart?

6. This week we explored God's design for marriage. On page 165 we read, "We live in a broken world that has desecrated marriage. Just because sinful humans have fractured the institution, that doesn't mean God's beautiful design was wrong or doesn't work. The Lord desires for us to know that His purpose for marriage is to bless us.

When redeemed men and women live according to God's design, then marriage showcases His glory to the world. Marriage conducted God's way is a magnificent demonstration of the grace that unites us with Christ." (Day 4)

- ❊ How would you describe the institution of marriage in our culture today?
- ❊ Read Ephesians 5:21-33 aloud, and work through the questions on pages 166–67 together:
  - What does verse 21 call both husbands and wives to do?
  - What do verses 22-24 call wives to do? Why?
  - According to verses 25-29, what are husbands to do? Be specific.
  - Verse 31 gives us the biblical definition for marriage. What is it?
  - What does the mystery of the "one flesh" union represent?
  - What final commands are given to the husband and wife in verse 33?
- ❊ What questions does Ephesians 5:21-33 raise for you? How are the egalitarian and complementarian views on the roles in marriage similar and different? Which more closely aligns with your own views? with the view of your church or denomination, or both?
- ❊ Discuss what submission does not mean. How would you describe the mutual submission called for in verse 21?

7. One major area where we can show God's glory to the world is in our families. On page 174 we read, "Our God is a God of order. He positioned the family as the fabric of society. He placed parents as the authority over their children. Within this framework, a child learns to respect authority and ultimately to honor God. Natural consequences arise when this authority structure is broken. Children who disrespect parents become adults who disrespect authority and do not fear the Lord." (Day 5)

- ❊ How would you describe your relationship with your parents? If you're comfortable sharing, do you feel you honor them as Scripture commands? Why or why not? (page 173)

✴ What are some ways we can honor our parents regardless of our relationship?

✴ What is the difference between obeying your parents and honoring your parents? Is one more difficult than the other? Why?

✴ Why do you think God chose a family as a primary place to manifest His character?

8. "As we honor our parents, we honor God. We show Jesus that we love Him through our obedience, and we show our parents the grace that He has given us. Who knows? Perhaps an unbelieving parent will see the glory of Christ and turn to Him in repentance. Perhaps through your obedience, a rift in the family could be healed. It's amazing how one act of obedience can transform someone's destiny." (Day 5)

✴ If you're comfortable sharing, what are some positive attributes of your parents? What are three positive attributes or characteristics your parent(s) passed on to you? (page 178)

✴ When as an adult have you sought counsel from your mom or dad? What wisdom did they provide?

✴ How could honoring a parent, even an unbelieving parent, lead him or her to repentance?

9. Think about all of your study and reflection this week.

✴ What thoughts or discoveries are sticking with you from this week's study?

Deeper Conversation (10 minutes)
Divide into smaller groups of two or three for deeper conversation. (Encourage the women to break into different groups each week.) Before the session, write on a markerboard or chart paper the question you want the groups to discuss:

✴ What is the evidence that you are filled with the Spirit? What aspect of your character changes when He is in control? (page 163)

Give a two-minute warning before time is up so that the groups may wrap up their discussion.

Video (30–35 minutes)

Play the Session 6 video segment on the DVD. Invite participants to complete the Video Viewer Guide for Session 6 in the participant workbook as they watch (page 179).

Choose one or two questions to help you briefly share thoughts or highlights from the video:

❖ What does it mean to stand firm in the face of a battle?

❖ How can we do this?

Closing Prayer (5 minutes)

Close the session by taking personal prayer requests from group members and leading the group in prayer. Invite members to participate in the Closing Prayer by praying out loud for one another and the requests given.

SESSION 7

Note: Because there is no video in this final session, there are some slight variations in format.

Leader Prep

Overview

Welcome to our final group session of *For His Glory: Living as God's Masterpiece*. Today we will review and discuss the lessons for Week 6 and discuss our main takeaways from the study.

In the lessons for Week 6, we learned about our victorious position as children of God. We discovered the reality of our salvation and all that Jesus accomplished for us on the cross. We learned how to walk worthy of our calling as God's masterpiece and showcase God's glory in the world. Finally, we learned to "stand firm" in our victorious position and not give sway to the schemes of the enemy. We explored the various pieces of the spiritual armor granted to us in Christ and how we can resist the spiritual forces of darkness that oppose us, gaining practical tools to help us resist the enemy and stand as God's masterpiece.

Main Point

To explore the tools that help us resist the enemy and stand as God's masterpiece.

Key Scriptures

10Be strong in the Lord and in the strength of his might. 11Put on the whole armor of God, that you may be able to stand against the schemes of the devil. 12For we do not wrestle against flesh and blood, but against the rulers, against the authorities, against the cosmic powers over this present darkness, against the spiritual forces of evil in the heavenly places. 13Therefore take up the whole armor of God, that you may be able to withstand in the evil day, and having done all, to stand firm.

[14] Stand therefore, having fastened on the belt of truth, and having put on the breastplate of righteousness, [15] and, as shoes for your feet, having put on the readiness given by the gospel of peace. [16] In all circumstances take up the shield of faith, with which you can extinguish all the flaming darts of the evil one; [17] and take the helmet of salvation, and the sword of the Spirit, which is the word of God.
(EPHESIANS 6:10-17)

What You Will Need

* ✳ *For His Glory* DVD and a DVD player
* ✳ Markerboard or chart paper and markers
* ✳ Stick-on name tags and markers (optional)
* ✳ iPod, smartphone, or tablet and portable speaker (optional)

Session Outline

Welcome and Opening Prayer (2 minutes)

To create a warm, welcoming environment as the women are gathering before the session begins, consider lighting one or more candles, providing coffee or other refreshments, and/or playing worship music. (Bring an iPod, smartphone, or tablet and a portable speaker if desired.) Be sure to provide name tags if the women do not know one another or you have new participants in your group. Then, when you are ready to begin, pray the following thematic prayer one last time, or offer your own prayer:

Gracious and beautiful God, thank You for the beauty that is all around us. Thank You for creating mountains and oceans and desert skies and sunsets over the ocean. With the same love, creativity, attention, and affection, You created each one of us. You call us Your masterpiece. Help us to understand what it means to live as a masterpiece, created by the Creator of the universe. Show us Your glory and teach us to live for Your glory alone. Amen.

Icebreaker (3 minutes)

Invite the women to share short, "popcorn" responses to the following question:

✤ What are you most afraid of—whether rationally or irrationally?

Group Discussion (20–35 minutes, depending on session length)

Note: More material is provided than you will have time to include. Before the session, select what you want to cover, putting a check mark beside it in your book. Page references are provided for those questions that relate to specific questions or activities in the participant workbook. For these questions, invite participants to share the answers they wrote in their books.

1. In regard to our battle against spiritual forces of evil, we read on page 184, "One thing we have celebrated in our study of Ephesians is the fact that through Christ's death and resurrection, He shattered the enemy's hold on us. Jesus 'delivered us from the domain of darkness and transferred us to the kingdom of his beloved Son' (Colossians 1:13). We are now seated victoriously with Christ. We don't fight *for* victory but *from* a place of victory. Knowing the difference is a game changer." (Day 1)

    ✤ What is the difference between fighting *for* victory and fighting *from* a place of victory?

    ✤ Read Ephesians 6:10-17. What is the battle that we are fighting?

    ✤ What does the word *scheme* bring to mind? (page 184) As you review the list on pages 185–86, what is one scheme you have personally experienced? Share how this tactic worked in your life to pull you away from Jesus or weakened your ability to glorify Him. (page 186)

    ✤ How does God equip us for the battle against the enemies' schemes?

2. This week we considered that "spiritual warfare comes in many forms and proves unique to each person." (Day 1)

    ✤ How does spiritual warfare show up in your life?

    ❧ Have you discovered any patterns that can help you fight it before you become overwhelmed by it?

    ❧ In what ways does the enemy attack our thought life? When and how have you battled thoughts that condemn, bring anxiety, accuse, or sow seeds of doubt?

3. One of the best ways to extinguish the fiery darts of the enemy is to take hold of the truth of the gospel and use it as an offensive weapon against the darkness that surrounds us. (Day 2)

    ❧ How can worship help us overcome the hold of the enemy on our thoughts?

    ❧ What are the six pieces of the armor of God? How does each protect or defend us from the evil one? (Refer to your notes on pages 190–92.)

    ❧ How can we use truth and righteousness and faith and peace and the Spirit as weapons against the spiritual forces of evil in this world?

4. Read aloud this excerpt from pages 192–93: "When a woman's soul is at peace, she knows her status before God is secure. She knows she is His masterpiece in whom He delights. She recognizes that this world is filled with trouble and heartache, but her God has overcome the world. This confidence brings security to every aspect of her being; and in the midst of life's trials, she knows that she belongs to Jesus. It is the peace of Christ that floods her heart when she remembers that nothing in this world can separate her from God's love." (Day 2)

    ❧ What does this mean?

    ❧ Does this description fit your current reality? Why or why not?

    ❧ What can you do to stand more firmly on your identity as a child of God?

5. Ephesians 6:16 refers to the "flaming arrows of the evil one" (NIV). On page 195 we read, "Although we don't face physical fiery darts, we do experience them in the spiritual realm. These fiery darts could be an

onslaught of temptation or an intense struggle with an addiction. They also could be sudden attacks of doubt or an extreme struggle with jealousy, pride, insecurity, or anger. Fiery darts often take the form of mental assaults that hurl themselves against our minds." (Day 3)

✳ What piece of spiritual armor protects against the fiery arrows of the enemy?

✳ Describe some flaming arrows that the enemy tries to heave at you.

✳ What can you do to take up your arms—your shield and your sword—against the enemy?

6. On page 196 we find this encouragement: "Faith holds fast to who God is. Although we can't see Him, we trust His character. When we lift up our shield of faith, we proclaim the greatness of our God to our own hearts and to the spiritual forces that oppose us." (Day 3)

✳ Think of a battle you're currently facing. What specific truth about God can you lift high (like a shield) that will extinguish the flaming arrows of the evil one? (page **196**)

✳ What are some ways that God has proven His character to you?

✳ What can we do to trust God's power, provision, and goodness more fully in every situation?

7. God invites us to come boldly into His presence. This access to God is our inheritance in Christ. On page **201** we read, "Prayer is our privilege! We are both wanted and welcomed." (Day 4)

✳ Do you feel wanted and welcomed by God? Why or why not? (page 201)

✳ What typically hinders you from coming into His presence? (page 201)

✳ What does it mean to you that the King of Glory invites you to come boldly into His presence any time, any day, any place?

✳ How might your prayer life change or be enriched if you began to believe, or believe even more fully, that you are both wanted and welcomed by God?

8. Prayer is integrally connected to our relationship with Jesus. On pages 203–04 we read, "Our power to overcome the enemy and walk in victory, living as God's glorious masterpiece, is found in our abiding relationship with Jesus. We are invited into a real relationship where we can walk with God and experience His power and presence. Prayer is the means in which we do so." (Day 4)

    ✻ Read Philippians 4:6-7. When are we to pray, and what result is promised to us when we pray? (page 203)

    ✻ If you truly believe God desires to hear from you and be with you, what would you like to share with Him in prayer? Or if you don't truly believe it just yet, what would you share if you did?

    ✻ How have you known the power of prayer in your own life?

9. On page 206 we find these beautiful words: "As we continually turn our thoughts back to the beauty of the cross, the triumph of God's grace, and the glory of Jesus, then we grow to love Him more deeply and walk with Him more intimately. Truly, this epistle fans to flame a passion for God's glory like none other." (Day 5)

    ✻ How has Paul's Letter to the Ephesians turned your thoughts back to the beauty of the cross?

    ✻ How has your study of this epistle led you to love Christ more deeply and walk with Him more intimately?

10. Think about all of your study and reflection this week.

    ✻ What thoughts or discoveries are sticking with you from this week's study?

Deeper Conversation (10 minutes)

Divide into smaller groups of two or three for deeper conversation. (Encourage the women to break into different groups each week.) Before the session, write on a markerboard or chart paper the question or questions you want the groups to discuss:

✷ How can we love Jesus in such a way that our passion for Him never fades, corrupts, or grows stale?

Give a two-minute warning before time is up so that the groups may wrap up their discussion.

Final Sharing (10–20 minutes, depending on session length)

As a full group, share your biggest takeaways from this study by discussing the following:

✷ How has this study changed the way you view yourself and others? Is it easier to think of yourself, and others, as God's masterpiece now than it was at the beginning of the study? Explain your response.

✷ What are you taking from this study that will help you live for His glory?

✷ What will it look like for *you* to live for God's glory?

Closing Prayer (5–10 minutes, depending on session length)

Close the session by taking personal prayer requests from group members and leading the group in prayer. Pray for one another and the requests given or, if you prefer, simply pray for each woman by name. Then read aloud Ephesians 3:20-21 as a closing benediction to your time together:

20Now to him who is able to do immeasurably more than all we ask or imagine, according to his power that is at work within us, 21to him be glory in the church and in Christ Jesus throughout all generations, for ever and ever! Amen.

(EPHESIANS 3:20-21 NIV)

For His
Glory

VIDEO VIEWER GUIDE ANSWERS

Session 1
Joy
royal announcement
status

Session 2
Hope
in Christ
glory

Session 3
saint
spiritually born
masterpiece

Session 4
position
surrender
loves Jesus
Holy Spirit

Session 5
look / gaze
love
forgiveness

Session 6
strong
armor
Stand firm

For His
Glory

60

GROUP ROSTER

Name **Phone** **Email**

_____ _____ _____

_____ _____ _____

_____ _____ _____

_____ _____ _____

_____ _____ _____

_____ _____ _____

_____ _____ _____

_____ _____ _____

_____ _____ _____

_____ _____ _____

_____ _____ _____

_____ _____ _____

_____ _____ _____

_____ _____ _____

_____ _____ _____

NOTES

_____

_____

_____

_____

_____

_____

_____

_____

_____

_____

_____

_____

_____

_____

_____

_____

CPSIA information can be obtained
at www.ICGtesting.com
Printed in the USA
LVHW060011131121
703202LV00001B/3